MONIQUE DILLARD

from
Open Gate

Diamond TRADITIONS

11 Multifaceted Quilts

Easy Piecing

Fat-Quarter Friendly

C&T PUBLISHING

Text copyright © 2013 by Monique Dillard

Photography and Artwork copyright © 2013 by C&T Publishing, Inc.

Publisher: Amy Marson

Creative Director: Gailen Runge

Art Director: Kristy Zacharias

Editors: Lynn Koolish and Jill Mordick

Technical Editors: Mary E. Flynn and Sandy Peterson

Cover Designers: Kristen Yenche and April Mostek

Book Designer: Kerry Graham

Production Coordinator: Jessica Jenkins

Production Editor: Alice Mace Nakanishi

Illustrator: Valyrie Friedman

Photo Assistant: Mary Peyton Peppo

Photography by Christina Carty-Francis and Diane Pedersen of C&T Publishing, Inc., unless otherwise noted

Published by C&T Publishing, Inc., P.O. Box 1456, Lafayette, CA 94549

Library of Congress Cataloging-in-Publication Data

Dillard, Monique, 1967-

 Diamond traditions : 11 multifaceted quilts - easy piecing - fat-quarter friendly / Monique Dillard.

  pages cm

 ISBN 978-1-60705-705-5 (soft cover)

1. Patchwork--Patterns. 2. Quilting--Patterns. 3. Quilts--Patterns. I. Title.

 TT835.D5479 2013

 746.46--dc23

                    2012042246

Printed in China

10 9 8 7 6 5 4 3 2 1

Acknowledgments

When I am working on a new book, I rely heavily on my wonderful friends to help me complete the projects. I would like to thank them for all their help and support as well as their love and encouragement.

Many thanks go to my wonderful and talented friends Joyce Davis, Peggy Drake, Kathy Rosecrance, Sue Glorch, Lynn Ohlendorf, and Thelma Childers, who helped me piece the quilts in this book; to LeAnne Olson, Danette Gonzalez, and Sue Glorch, who provided the creative machine quilting; and to proofreaders Kathy Rosecrance and Thelma Childers.

Thanks go to Maywood Studio for supplying me with Memories of Provence, my second fabric line, and also thanks to Moda for always providing me with their wonderful fabric. Thanks to Riley Blake for generously sending me fabric for two of the quilts in this book and to RJR Fabrics for providing me with fabric. Lastly, I would like to express my appreciation to C&T Publishing for publishing my books and their helpful and professional staff.

Contents

Introduction   4

General Instructions   5

PROJECTS

Black Diamond   11

Diamond in the Rough   16

Diamonds and Pearls   20

Marquis   25

Square Cut   29

Diamonds Are Forever   34

Diamond Eyes   38

Ocean of Diamonds   43

Radiance   49

Blue Heart Diamond   53

Brilliance   57

Quiltmaking Basics   60

About the Author   63

Resources   63

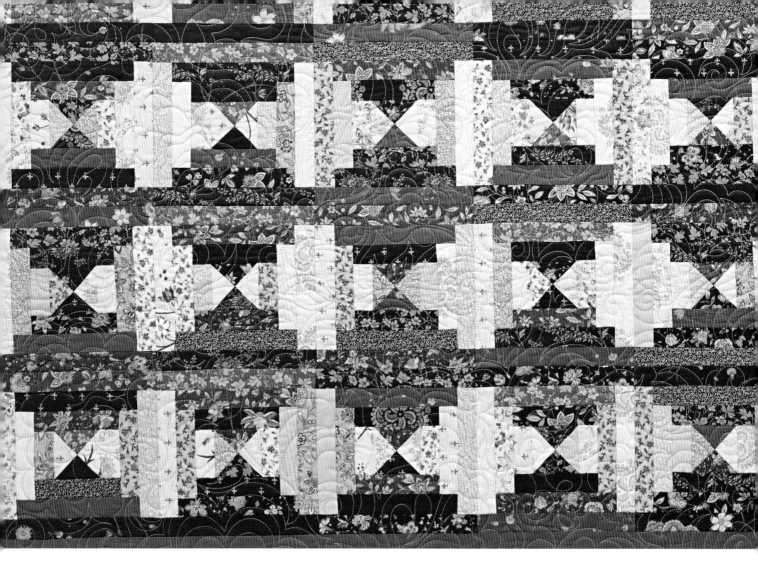

Introduction

You know the old saying "Diamonds are a girl's best friend"? Even though I like diamonds, I much prefer quilts. I named the quilts in this book after diamonds because when I was working on these quilts, I noticed how many of them have diamond shapes. Some of the quilts such as *Black Diamond* (page 11) have obvious diamonds; in other quilts, such as *Diamond in the Rough* (page 16), the diamonds are much less obvious.

As in my last two books with C&T Publishing, *Fat Quarter Winners* and *Traditional Fat Quarter Quilts*, the quilts in this book are made with fat quarters—some quilts feature fat quarters as backgrounds and others use fat quarters as the main feature. Sometimes I like the scrappiness of a fat-quarter background; other times the cohesiveness of a single background has great appeal. It was fun using both.

Also, as in my previous two books, you have the option of using my Fit to be Square (page 9) and Fit to be Geese (page 7) rulers. For this book I added another of my rulers, the Fit to be Quarter. It is designed to trim quarter-square triangles (page 10) and combination units (page 6). The rulers are easy to use and provide accurate results but are not required for any of the patterns in the book.

I hope you enjoy creating these diamond-themed fat-quarter quilts as much as I did!

General Instructions

This chapter contains the instructions for making the commonly used block components in this book: half-square triangle units made with traditional construction, combination units, Flying Geese units, square-in-a-square units, and quarter-square triangle units. The last four can be made using either traditional construction or optional specialty rulers. Additional instructions are included with the rulers.

half-square triangle units

Draw a diagonal line from corner to corner on the back of the lighter square. Match a light square with a dark square, right sides together. Sew ¼″ from both sides of the line. Cut the pieces apart on the line and press toward the darker triangle. Note that in the directions, half-square triangle units are made larger than needed so you can square them to the exact size.

combination units

traditional method

1. Sew a square to a rectangle. Repeat. Press in the direction of the arrows. Rotate one unit and sew the pair together. (Watch the placement of the squares.) On the back of the piece, snip ¼″ in the center seam so that you can press half of the seam up and the other half down.

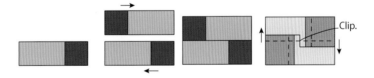

2. On the back of the unit from Step 1, use the 45° mark on your ruler to draw 2 diagonal lines. Note that one line starts at the upper left corner and the other line starts at the lower right corner. The lines must be at a 45° angle and cross where your seams meet. Place the unit right sides together on an unpieced rectangle. Sew exactly on the lines and cut ¼″ in from the lines. (Before cutting, check to make sure the sewn lines are in the correct direction.) Press in the directions of the arrows.

fit to be quarter method

1. Sew a square to a rectangle. Repeat. Press in the direction of the arrows. Rotate one unit and sew the pair together. (Watch the placement of the squares.) On the back of the piece, snip ¼″ in the center seam so that you can press half of the seam up and the other half down.

2. On the backs of the unit from Step 1, use the 45° mark on your ruler to draw 2 diagonal lines. Note that one line starts at the upper left corner and the other line starts at the lower right corner. The lines must be at a 45° angle and cross where your seams meet. Place the unit right sides together on an unpieced rectangle. Sew exactly on the lines and cut ¼″ in from the lines. (Before cutting, check to make sure the sewn lines are in the correct direction.) Press in the direction of the arrows.

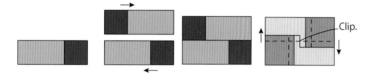

3. Square by lining up the square to half of the unfinished size of the piece. Make sure the diagonal line is along the unfinished size of the piece. Trim the 2 sides. Rotate 180° and line up the piece on the unfinished size. Trim.

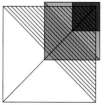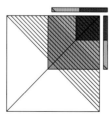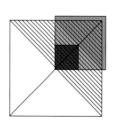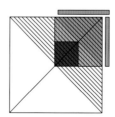

flying geese units

traditional flying geese method

1. On the backs of 2 squares, draw a diagonal line from corner to corner.

Draw line.

2. Place a square on one end of the rectangle, right sides together. Sew directly on the line, and press in the direction of the arrow. You now have 3 layers of fabric in the corner. Trim the 2 underneath layers to ¼". Place the other square with a drawn line right sides together on the opposite end of the rectangle. The second square will overlap the first square by ¼". Sew directly on the line and press in the direction of the arrow. Trim the 2 underneath layers to ¼".

fit to be geese method

1. Cut a square diagonally once to create 2 triangles.

2. Cut a second, larger square diagonally twice to create 4 triangles.

3. Sew the long side of a triangle from Step 1 to the short side of a triangle from Step 2. Press in the direction of the arrow. Sew a matching triangle from Step 1 to the other short side of the triangle from Step 2. Press in the direction of the arrow.

4. Align the rooftop of the ruler along the seams and trim the top of the Flying Geese unit using the Fit to be Geese ruler. Rotate the fabric 180° and align the trimmed edge with the horizontal line showing the size of Flying Geese unit that you are making. Trim the untrimmed edge. Rotate the piece 90°. Align the trimmed top and bottom edges of the unit with the red lines for the correct size on the ruler. Make sure that the center red dashed line is lined up where the seams cross, and then trim. (Use the dashed red line that is ¼" above the correct-sized

black line.) Rotate the piece 180° and trim the other side by again aligning the piece with the red dashes showing the correct size and the red dashed line in the center where the seams cross.

Trim.

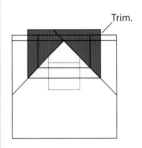

Trim.

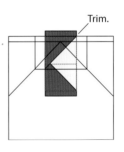

Trim.

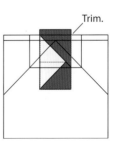

Trim.

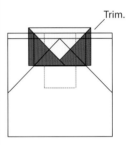

square-in-a-square units

traditional square-in-a-square method

1. Cut 2 squares diagonally once to create 4 triangles.

2. Sew 2 triangles from Step 1 to the opposite sides of another square. Press toward the triangles. Sew 2 more of the triangles from Step 1 to the top and bottom of the square. Press toward the triangles.

fit to be square method

1. Cut 2 squares diagonally once to create 4 triangles.

2. Sew 2 triangles from Step 1 to the opposite sides of a square. Press toward the triangles. Sew 2 more of the triangles from Step 1 to the top and bottom of the square. Press toward the triangles.

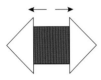

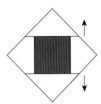

3. Align the rooftop of the ruler along the seam, making sure that the vertical line runs through the seam intersection at the bottom, and trim the top of the square-in-a-square unit. Rotate the piece 180° and again align the rooftop along the seam while aligning the cut edge along the correct block size. Trim. Rotate the piece 90°. Align the rooftop along the seam and the vertical line on the bottom where the seams cross. Note that the sides should fall along the correct size for your block. Trim. Rotate 180°; align the rooftop, the bottom measurement, and the sides. Trim.

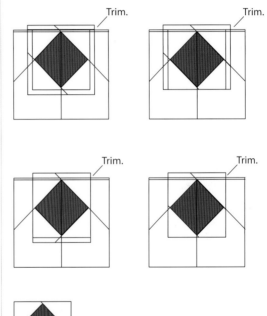

quarter-square triangle units

traditional quarter-square triangle method

Match a square (D) with a square (E). On the back of the square (D), draw a diagonal line from corner to corner. Sew ¼" out from both sides of the drawn line. Cut directly on the line. Press toward the triangle (E). Rotate one unit 180° and place it right sides together with the second unit, with contrasting triangles placed face-to-face. On the back of one unit, draw a diagonal line from corner to corner. Sew ¼" from both sides of the drawn line. Cut directly on the line. Press in the direction of the arrows.

fit to be quarter method

1. Match a square (D) with a square (E). On the backs of the square (D), draw a diagonal line from corner to corner. Sew ¼" from both sides of the drawn line. Cut directly on the line. Press toward the triangle (E). Rotate one unit 180° and place it right sides together with the second unit, with contrasting triangles placed face-to-face. On the back of one unit, draw a diagonal line from corner to corner. Sew ¼" from both sides of the drawn line. Cut directly on the line. Press in the direction of the arrows.

2. Using the Fit to be Quarter ruler, align with the line for the size that you need and the center of the quarter-square triangle with half the unfinished size. For example, if you are trimming a 4" square, line up the 2" lines in the center and the 4" where the seams cross at the top and side. Trim. Rotate 180° and align the 4" lines on the edges that you just cut. Trim.

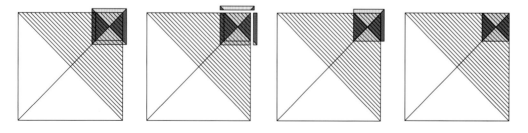

Black Diamond

Designed and made by Monique Dillard

Quilted by LeAnne Olson

Fabric: Batiks from Hoffman Fabrics

FINISHED BLOCK: 8″ × 14″

FINISHED QUILT: 41″ × 65″
(25 full blocks, 12 half-blocks, and 4 quarter-blocks)

materials

- **Black fabric:** 8 fat quarters
- **Gold fabric:** 8 fat quarters
- **Outer border:** 1 yard
- **Binding:** ½ yard
- **Backing:** 3 yards
- **Batting:** 51″ × 75″
- **Quilter's ruler:** 6″ × 24″

cutting instructions

BLACK FAT QUARTERS:

From each black fat quarter:

Cut 4 strips 1½″ × width of fabric; cut into 4 pieces 1½″ × 17″ (A).

Cut 4 strips 1½″ × width of fabric; cut into 4 pieces 1½″ × 13″ (B) and 4 pieces 1½″ × 7″ (D).

Cut 2 strips 1½″ × width of fabric; cut into 4 pieces 1½″ × 10″ (C).

GOLD FAT QUARTERS:

From each gold fat quarter:

Cut 4 strips 1½″ × width of fabric; cut into 4 pieces 1½″ × 17″ (E).

Cut 4 strips 1½″ × width of fabric; cut into 4 pieces 1½″ × 13″ (F) and 4 pieces 1½″ × 7″ (H).

Cut 2 strips 1½″ × width of fabric; cut into 4 pieces 1½″ × 10″ (G).

OUTER BORDER:

Cut 6 strips 5″ × width of fabric.

BINDING:

Cut 6 strips 2½″ × width of fabric.

piecing

Seam allowances are ¼".

1. Sew 2 of the black 1½" × 17" pieces (A) together. Press in one direction. Repeat to make 16.

A
A

Make 16.

2. Center and sew a black 1½" × 13" piece (B) to both sides of a unit from Step 1. Press in the direction of the arrows. Repeat to make 16.

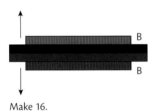

B
B

Make 16.

3. Center and sew a black 1½" × 10" piece (C) to both sides of a unit from Step 2. Press in the direction of the arrows. Repeat to make 16.

C
C

Make 16.

4. Center and sew a black 1½" × 7" piece (D) to both sides of a unit from Step 3. Press in the direction of the arrows. Repeat to make 16.

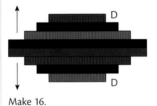

D
D

Make 16.

5. Placing the ruler as shown, as close to the top left edge as you can and using the 30° angle on your ruler, trim the top left diagonal edge of a unit from Step 4, lining up the center seam with the 30° angle. Rotate the ruler and, again using the 30° angle on your ruler, trim the adjacent top diagonal edge of the unit to create a point. Rotate the unit 180°. From one side, measure perpendicular from side-to-side to 7½". Trim. Rotate the ruler and repeat for the other side. Repeat to make 16.

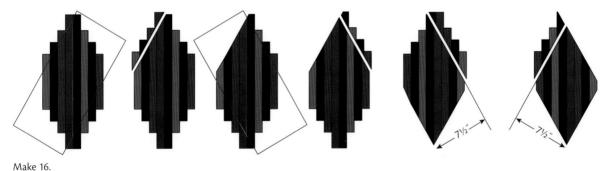

Make 16.

6. Sew 2 of the gold 1½" × 17" pieces (E) together. Press in one direction. Repeat to make 12.

Make 12.

7. Center and sew a gold 1½" × 13" piece (F) to both sides of the pieces from Step 6. Press in the direction of the arrows. Repeat to make 12.

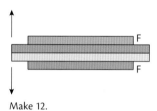

Make 12.

8. Center and sew a gold 1½" × 10" piece (G) to both sides of the pieces from Step 7. Press in the direction of the arrows. Repeat to make 12.

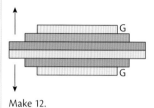

Make 12.

9. Center and sew a gold 1½" × 7" piece (H) to both sides of the pieces from Step 8. Press in the direction of the arrows. Repeat to make 12.

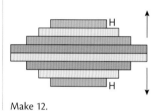

Make 12.

10. Placing the ruler as shown, as close to the top left edge as you can, and using the 30° angle on your ruler, trim the top left diagonal edge of a unit from Step 9, lining up the center seam with the 30° angle. Rotate the ruler and, again using the 30° angle on your ruler, trim the unit to create a point. Rotate the unit 180°. From one side, measure perpendicular from side-to-side to 7½" and trim. Rotate the ruler and repeat for the other side. Repeat to make 9. Reserve the remaining three units for Step 11.

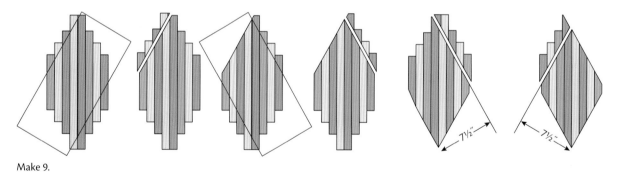

Make 9.

11. Use the 30° angle on your ruler to trim a piece from Step 9, aligning the center seam with the 30° angle. Rotate the ruler and, again using the 30° angle on your ruler, trim the piece at the top to create a point. From one side, measure across to 8¼" and trim. Rotate and repeat for the other side. Cut the pieces in half horizontally. Repeat with the remaining units. These are the 6 top and bottom half-blocks.

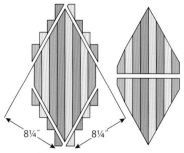

Make 6 for top and bottom.

12. Sew a gold 1½″ × 17″ piece (E) to a gold 1½″ × 13″ piece (F). Sew on a gold 1½″ × 10″ piece (G) and then a gold 1½″ × 7″ piece (H). Press in the direction of the arrows. Repeat to make 8.

Make 8.

13. Use the 30° angle on the ruler to trim the top right edge of a unit from Step 12. Rotate the ruler and trim the bottom right edge of the unit in the same way. Repeat on a second unit from Step 12. Cut each in half for 4 corners.

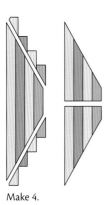

Make 4.

14. For the 6 remaining units from Step 12, use the 30° angle on the ruler to trim the top right edge. Rotate the ruler and trim the bottom right edge of the unit in the same way, beginning 15¾″ down from the top trimmed edge. These are the side units.

Make 6.

quilt construction

Refer to the quilt photo (page 11) and to the quilt assembly diagram (below). See Borders (page 60) for information on making the borders.

1. Arrange your quilt in diagonal rows and sew the diamonds into rows. Press in the direction of the arrows. Join the rows and press in one direction. Trim the top and bottom to ¼″ seams. Sew on the outer border. Press toward the outer border.

2. Quilt, bind, and enjoy!

Quilt assembly diagram

Diamond in the Rough

Designed by Monique Dillard

Made by Joyce Davis

Quilted by Danette Gonzalez

Fabric: Grandma's House by The Paper Loft for Riley Blake Designs

FINISHED BLOCK: 10½″ × 10½″

FINISHED QUILT: 55″ × 65½″ (20 blocks)*

* See additional information for alternate quilt sizes on page 19.

materials

- **Main light fabric:** 1½ yards
- **Brown fabric:** 7 fat quarters
- **Green fabric:** 7 fat quarters
- **Inner border:** ¼ yard
- **Outer border:** 1¼ yards
- **Binding:** ⅝ yard
- **Backing:** 3¾ yards
- **Batting:** 65″ × 76″

cutting instructions

Each brown and green fat-quarter pair along with the main light makes 3 blocks.

MAIN LIGHT FABRIC:
From the main light fabric:

Cut 11 strips 2½″ × width of fabric; cut into 168 squares 2½″ × 2½″ (A).

Cut 11 strips 2″ × width of fabric; cut into 84 pieces 2″ × 5″ (D).

BROWN FAT QUARTERS:
From each brown fat quarter:

Cut 3 strips 2½″ × width of fabric; cut into 24 squares 2½″ × 2½″ (B).

Cut 3 strips 2″ × width of fabric for strip piecing.

GREEN FAT QUARTERS:
From each green fat quarter:

Cut 3 strips 2″ × width of fabric for strip piecing.

Cut 2 strips 2″ × width of fabric; cut into 15 squares 2″ × 2″ (C).

INNER BORDER:
Cut 5 strips 1½″ × width of fabric.

OUTER BORDER:
Cut 6 strips 6″ × width of fabric.

BINDING:
Cut 7 strips 2½″ × width of fabric.

piecing

Seam allowances are ¼″.

1. Sew a brown strip 2″ × width of fabric and a green strip 2″ × width of fabric together. Press toward the brown. Make 3 strip sets per brown and green pair. Subcut into 24 segments 2″ wide. Pair up 2 segments; rotate one segment and sew to the other to create a Four-Patch. Press in the direction of the arrow. Repeat for a total of 12.

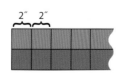

Make 3 strip sets and 12 Four-Patch units per brown and green pair.

2. Make 48 half-square triangles using 24 main light 2½″ × 2½″ squares (A) and 24 brown 2½″ × 2½″ squares (B). Refer to Half-Square Triangle Units (*page 5*). Press toward the brown. Square to 2″ × 2″. Make 48 for each brown.

Make 48 per brown.

3. Sew the half-square triangles together. Make 12 per brown.

Make 12 per brown.

4. Sew the half-square triangles together. Make 12 per brown.

Make 12 per brown.

5. Sew together the pieces from Step 1, Step 3, and Step 4 with a green 2″ × 2″ square (C). Press in the direction of the arrows. Square the piece to 5″ × 5″. Repeat to make 12.

Make 12.

6. Sew the block together using the pieces from Step 5, a green 2″ × 2″ square (C), and the main light 2″ × 5″ pieces (D). Square to 11″ × 11″. Repeat the entire procedure to make the total number of blocks needed for your desired quilt size. (For the project quilt, page 16, make 20 blocks. You will have an extra block.)

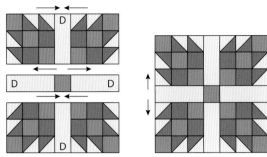

Make 3 per brown and green pair for a total of 21.

quilt construction

Refer to the quilt photo (page 16) and to the quilt assembly diagram (below). See Borders (page 60) for information on making the borders.

1. Arrange and sew your quilt in rows. Rotate the blocks so that the seams are headed in opposite directions. Press in the direction of the arrows. Sew on the inner and outer borders. Press toward the borders.

2. Quilt, bind, and enjoy!

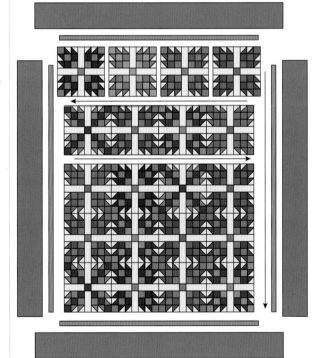

Quilt assembly diagram

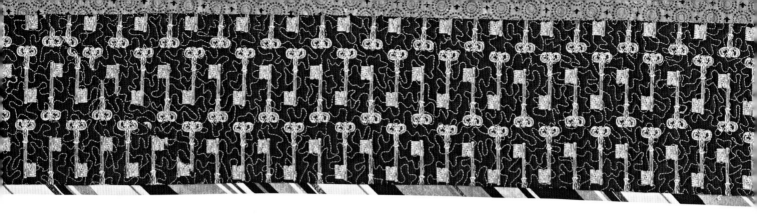

alternate quilt sizes

	Twin	Full/Queen	King
Number of blocks	35*	56*	81
Number of blocks wide × long	5 × 7	7 × 8	9 × 9
Finished size	65½″ × 86½″	86½″ × 97″	107½″ × 107½″
Yardage			
Main light	2½	3¾	5¼
Brown fat quarters	12	19	27
Green fat quarters	12	19	27
Inner border	⅓	½	½
Outer border	1½	1⅔	2
Binding	¾	⅞	1
Backing	5⅝	8⅛	9⅞
Batting	76″ × 96″	96″ × 107″	117″ × 117″
Main light cutting			
Number of strips × width of fabric Number of squares (A)	18 strips 2½″ 288 squares 2½″ × 2½″	29 strips 2½″ 456 squares 2½″ × 2½″	41 strips 2½″ 648 squares 2½″ × 2½″
Number of strips × width of fabric Number of pieces (D)	18 strips 2″ 144 pieces 2″ × 5″	29 strips 2″ 228 pieces 2″ × 5″	41 strips 2″ 324 pieces 2″ × 5″

* You will have extra blocks.

Diamonds and Pearls

Designed and made by Monique Dillard

Quilted by LeAnne Olson

Fabric: St. Remy de Provence by Robyn Pandolph for RJR Fabrics

FINISHED BLOCK: 7½″ × 7½″

FINISHED QUILT: 56″ × 71″ (48 blocks)*

* See additional information for alternate quilt sizes on page 24.

materials

- **Main light fabric:** 2¼ yards
- **Pink fabric:** 6 fat quarters
- **Black fabric:** 6 fat quarters
- **Outer border:** 1¼ yards
- **Binding:** ⅝ yard
- **Backing:** 3⅞ yards
- **Batting:** 66″ × 81″
- **Optional:** Fit to be Quarter ruler

cutting instructions

Before beginning, match your pink and black fat quarters in pairs for piecing. Each pair along with the main light fabric makes 8 blocks.

MAIN LIGHT FABRIC:
From the main light fabric:

- **Fit to be Quarter Method (page 6)**

Cut 10 strips 3½″ × width of fabric; cut into 192 pieces 2″ × 3½″ (I).

Cut 8 strips 2¼″ × width of fabric; cut into 96 pieces 2¼″ × 3¼″ (D).

Cut 10 strips 2″ × width of fabric; cut into 192 squares 2″ × 2″ (H).

- **Traditional Method (page 5)**

Cut 10 strips 3½″ × width of fabric; cut into 192 pieces 3½″ × 2″ (I).

Cut 8 strips 2″ × width of fabric; cut into 96 pieces 2″ × 3″ (D).

Cut 10 strips 2″ × width of fabric; cut into 192 squares 2″ × 2″ (H).

PINK FAT QUARTERS:
From each pink fat quarter:

- **Fit to be Quarter Method (page 6)**

Cut 1 strip 4″ × width of fabric; cut into 4 pieces 4″ × 5″ (G).

Cut 3 strips 2½″ × width of fabric; cut into 20 squares 2½″ × 2½″ (A).

Cut 1 strip 2¼″ × width of fabric; cut into 8 squares 2¼″ × 2¼″ (C).

- **Traditional Method (page 5)**

Cut 1 strip 3½″ × width of fabric; cut into 4 pieces 3½″ × 4½″ (G).

Cut 3 strips 2½″ × width of fabric; cut into 20 squares 2½″ × 2½″ (A).

Cut 1 strip 2″ × width of fabric; cut into 8 squares 2″ × 2″ (C).

BLACK FAT QUARTERS:

From each black fat quarter:

- **Fit to be Quarter Method (page 6)**

Cut 1 strip 4″ × width of fabric; cut into 4 pieces 4″ × 5″ (E).

Cut 3 strips 2½″ × width of fabric; cut into 20 squares 2½″ × 2½″ (B).

Cut 1 strip 2¼″ × width of fabric; cut into 8 squares 2¼″ × 2¼″ (F).

- **Traditional Method (page 5)**

Cut 1 strip 3½″ × width of fabric; cut into 4 pieces 3½″ × 4½″ (E).

Cut 3 strips 2½″ × width of fabric; cut into 20 squares 2½″ × 2½″ (B).

Cut 1 strip 2″ × width of fabric; cut into 8 squares 2″ × 2″ (F).

BORDER:

Cut 6 strips 6″ × width of fabric.

BINDING:

Cut 7 strips 2½″ × width of fabric.

piecing

Seam allowances are ¼″.

1. Make 40 half-square triangles per pair of fat quarters using 20 pink 2½″ squares (A) and 20 black 2½″ squares (B). Trim the squares to 2″ × 2″. Refer to Half-Square Triangle Units (page 5).

Make 40.

2. Sew the pieces together from Step 1 with main light 2″ × 2″ squares (H). Press in the direction of the arrows. Square the piece to 3½″ × 3½″. Repeat to make 16 per pink and black fat-quarter pair.

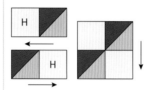

Make 16.

3. Fit to be Quarter Method: Make 8 combination units (page 6) for each fat-quarter pair using 8 main light 2¼″ × 3¼″ pieces (D), 8 pink 2¼″ × 2¼″ squares (C), and 4 black 4″ × 5″ pieces (E). Press in the direction of the arrows. Square to 3½″ × 3½″.

Traditional Method: Make 8 combination units (page 5) for each fat-quarter pair using 8 main light 2″ × 3″ pieces (D), 8 pink 2″ × 2″ squares (C), and 4 black 3½″ × 4½″ pieces (E). Press in the direction of the arrows. Square to 3½″ × 3½″.

Make 4 per pink fat quarter.

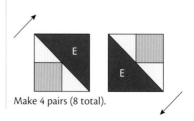

Make 4 pairs (8 total).

4. Fit to be Quarter Method: Make 8 combination units (page 6) for each fat-quarter pair using 8 main light 2¼″ × 3¼″ pieces (D), 8 black 2¼″ × 2¼″ squares (F), and 4 pink 4″ × 5″ pieces (G). Press in the direction of the arrows. Square to 3½″ × 3½″.

Traditional Method: Make 8 combination units (page 5) for each fat-quarter pair using 8 main light 2″ × 3″ pieces (D), 8 black 2″ × 2″ squares (F), and 4 pink 3½″ × 4½″ pieces (G). Press in the direction of the arrows. Square to 3½″ × 3½″.

Make 4 per black fat quarter.

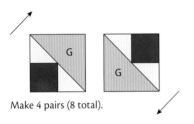

Make 4 pairs (8 total).

5. Sew the block together using the pieces from Step 2, Step 3, Step 4, main light pieces 2″ × 3½″ (I), and the remaining half-square triangles from Step 1. Square the block to 8″ × 8″. Repeat the entire procedure to make the total number of blocks needed for your desired quilt size. (For the project quilt, page 20, make 48 blocks.)

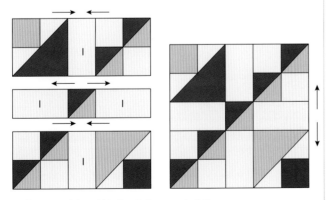

Make 8 per pink and black pair for a total of 48.

quilt construction

Refer to the quilt photo (page 20) and to the quilt assembly diagram (below). See Borders (page 60) for information on making the borders.

1. Arrange and sew your quilt in rows. Press in the direction of the arrows. Sew on the outer border. Press toward the outer border.

2. Quilt, bind, and enjoy!

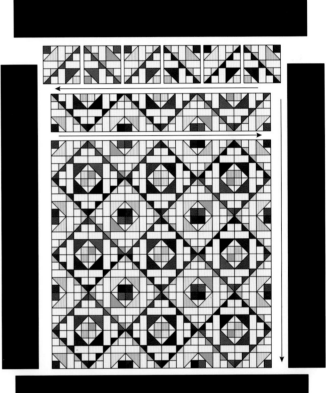

Quilt assembly diagram

alternate quilt sizes

	Twin	Full/Queen	King
Number of blocks	60*	120	196*
Number of blocks wide × long	6 × 10	10 × 12	14 × 14
Finished size	56″ × 86″	86″ × 101″	116″ × 116″
Yardage			
Main light	2⅝	5⅛	8⅓
Pink fat quarters	8	15	25
Black fat quarters	8	15	25
Border	1⅓	1⅞	2¼
Binding	⅝	⅞	1
Backing	5½	8⅛	10½
Batting	66″ × 96″	96″ × 111″	126″ × 126″
Main light cutting: Fit to be Quarter method			
Number of strips × width of fabric Number of rectangles (I)	12 strips 3½″ 240 pieces 3½″ × 2″	24 strips 3½″ 480 pieces 3½″ × 2″	40 strips 3½″ 784 pieces 3½″ × 2″
Number of strips × width of fabric Number of rectangles (D)	10 strips 2¼″ 120 pieces 2¼″ × 3¼″	20 strips 2¼″ 240 pieces 2¼″ × 3¼″	33 strips 2¼″ 392 pieces 2¼″ × 3¼″
Number of strips × width of fabric Number of squares (H)	12 strips 2″ 240 squares 2″ × 2″	24 strips 2″ 480 squares 2″ × 2″	40 strips 2″ 784 squares 2″ × 2″
Main light cutting: Traditional method			
Number of strips × width of fabric Number of rectangles (I)	12 strips 3½″ 240 pieces 3½″ × 2″	24 strips 3½″ 480 pieces 3½″ × 2″	40 strips 3½″ 784 pieces 3½″ × 2″
Number of strips × width of fabric Number of rectangles (D)	10 strips 2″ 120 pieces 2″ × 3″	19 strips 2″ 240 pieces 2″ × 3″	31 strips 2″ 392 pieces 2″ × 3″
Number of strips × width of fabric Number of squares (H)	12 strips 2″ 240 squares 2″ × 2″	24 strips 2″ 480 squares 2″ × 2″	40 strips 2″ 784 squares 2″ × 2″

* You will have extra blocks.

Marquis

Designed and made by Monique Dillard

Quilted by LeAnne Olson

Fabric: Rouenneries Deux by French General for Moda Fabrics

FINISHED BLOCK: 8½″ × 8½″

FINISHED QUILT: 68″ × 83″ (48 blocks)*

* See additional information for alternate quilt sizes on page 28.

materials

- **Light fabric:** 12 fat quarters

- **Dark fabric:** 12 fat quarters

- **Inner border and binding:** 2 yards

- **Outer border:** 1¾ yards

- **Backing:** 4¼ yards

- **Batting:** 78″ × 93″

- **Optional:** Fit to be Quarter ruler

cutting instructions

Each pair of light and dark fat quarters makes 4 blocks.

LIGHT FAT QUARTERS:

From each light fat quarter:

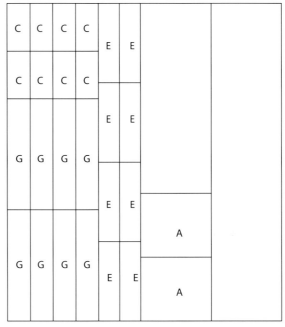

Light fat quarter

- **Fit to be Quarter Method (page 10)**

Cut 6 strips 1½″ × width of fabric; cut into 8 pieces
1½″ × 7″ (G), 8 pieces 1½″ × 5″ (E), and 8 pieces
1½″ × 3″ (C), per diagram.

Cut 1 strip 4″ × width of fabric; cut into 2 squares
4″ × 4″ cut diagonally twice (A).

- **Traditional Method (page 10)**

Cut 6 strips 1½″ × width of fabric; cut into 8 pieces
1½″ × 7″ (G), 8 pieces 1½″ × 5″ (E), and 8 pieces
1½″ × 3″ (C), per diagram.

Cut 1 strip 3¾″ × width of fabric; cut into 2 squares
3¾″ × 3¾″ cut diagonally twice (A).

DARK FAT QUARTERS:

From each dark fat quarter:

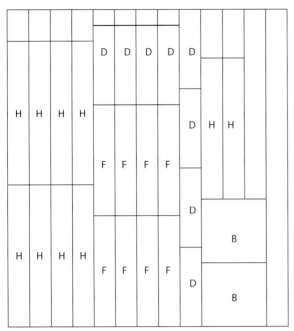

Dark fat quarter

- **Fit to be Quarter Method (page 10)**

Cut 9 strips 1½″ × width of fabric; cut into 8 pieces 1½″ × 9″ (H), 8 pieces 1½″ × 7″ (F), and 8 pieces 1½″ × 5″ (D), per diagram.

Cut 1 strip 4″ × width of fabric; cut into 2 squares 4″ × 4″ (B) and 2 pieces 1½″ × 9″ (H).

- **Traditional Method (page 10)**

Cut 9 strips 1½″ × width of fabric; cut into 8 pieces 1½″ × 9″ (H), 8 pieces 1½″ × 7″ (F), and 8 pieces 1½″ × 5″ (D), per diagram.

Cut 1 strip 3¾″ × width of fabric; cut into 2 squares 3¾″ × 3¾″ (B) and 2 pieces 1½″ × 9″ (H).

INNER BORDER AND BINDING:

Cut 8 strips 1½″ × width of fabric for inner border.

Cut 8 strips 2½″ × width of fabric for binding.

OUTER BORDER:

Cut 8 strips 7″ × width of fabric for outer border.

piecing

Seam allowances are ¼″.

1. Make 48 quarter-square triangles measuring 3″ × 3″ using the various lights and darks. The scrappy nature of this project makes the quick-pieced quarter-square triangle methods used elsewhere in this book unsuitable. You can still choose between the Traditional (actual size) and Fit to be Quarter (sew oversized and trim down) methods without first quick-piecing the triangles.

Fit to be Quarter Method (page 10): Use 96 light triangles cut from 4″ × 4″ squares cut diagonally twice (A) and 96 dark triangles cut from 4″ × 4″ squares cut diagonally twice (B).

Traditional Method (page 10): Use 96 light triangles cut from 3¾″ × 3¾″ squares cut diagonally twice (A) and 96 dark triangles cut from 3¾″ × 3¾″ squares cut diagonally twice (B).

Make 48.

2. Sew a light 1½″ × 3″ piece (C) to both sides of the light piece from Step 1. Press toward the light. Repeat to make 48.

Make 48.

3. Sew a dark 1½″ × 5″ piece (D) to the top and bottom of the piece from Step 2. Press toward the dark. Repeat to make 48.

Make 48.

4. Sew a light 1½″ × 5″ piece (E) to both sides of the piece from Step 3. Press toward the light. Repeat to make 48.

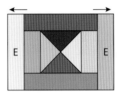

Make 48.

5. Sew a dark 1½″ × 7″ piece (F) to the top and bottom of the piece from Step 4. Press toward the dark. Repeat to make 48.

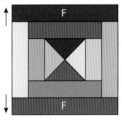

Make 48.

6. Sew a light 1½″ × 7″ piece (G) to both sides of the piece from Step 5. Press toward the light. Repeat to make 48.

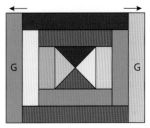

Make 48.

7. Sew a dark 1½" × 9" piece (H) to the top and bottom of the piece from Step 6. Press toward the dark. Repeat Steps 1–7 to make the total number of blocks needed for your desired quilt size. (For the project quilt, page 25, make 48 blocks.). *Note:* Use the remaining dark 1½" × 9" pieces (H) in Quilt Construction (below).

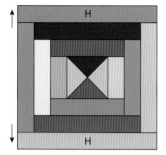

Make 48.

quilt construction

Refer to the quilt photo (page 25) and to the quilt assembly diagram (at right). See Borders (page 60) for information on making the borders.

1. Arrange and sew together the quilt in rows with the leftover dark 1½" × 9" pieces (H) on the sides of the rows. Press in the direction of the arrows.

2. Sew on the inner border and the outer border. Press toward the borders.

3. Quilt, bind, and enjoy!

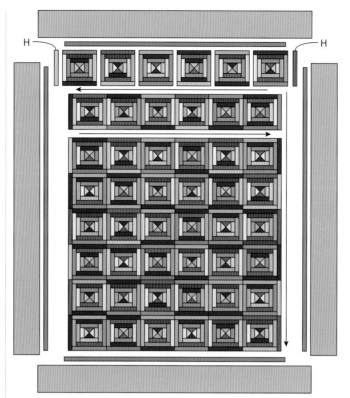

Quilt assembly diagram

alternate quilt sizes

	Full/Queen	King
Number of blocks	90	121
Number of blocks wide × long	9 × 10	11 × 11
Finished size	93½" × 110"	110½" × 108½"
Yardage		
Light fat quarters	23	31
Dark fat quarters	23	31
Inner border and binding	1⅓	1⅜
Outer border	2⅛	2⅜
Backing	8⅞	10¼
Batting	104" × 120"	121" × 119"

Square Cut

Designed by Monique Dillard

Made by Kathy Rosecrance

Quilted by LeAnne Olson

Fabric: Farmer's Market by Brannock & Patek for Moda Fabrics

FINISHED BLOCK: 16″ × 16″

FINISHED QUILT: 62½″ × 78½″ (12 blocks)*

* See additional information for alternate quilt sizes on page 33.

materials

- **Light fabric:** 2¼ yards
- **Medium fabric:** 12 fat quarters
- **Dark fabric:** 6 fat quarters
- **Inner border:** ⅜ yard
- **Outer border:** 1⅝ yards
- **Binding:** ⅝ yard
- **Backing:** 5⅛ yards
- **Batting:** 73″ × 89″

cutting instructions

Before beginning, match 2 medium fat quarters with 1 dark fat quarter for piecing. Cut all fat quarters separately. Each set of medium and half of the dark pieces along with the main light makes 4 quarter-blocks or 1 large block.

MAIN LIGHT FABRIC:
From the light fabric:

Cut 12 strips 3″ × width of fabric; cut into 144 squares 3″ × 3″ (A).

Cut 12 strips 2⅞″ × width of fabric; cut into 144 squares 2⅞″ × 2⅞″. Cut each diagonally once (C).

MEDIUM FAT QUARTERS:
From each medium fat quarter:

Cut 1 strip 4⅞″ × width of fabric; cut into 2 squares 4⅞″ × 4⅞″. Cut each diagonally once (D).

Cut 2 strips 3″ × width of fabric; cut into 12 squares 3″ × 3″ (B).

Cut 1 strip 2⅞″ × width of fabric; cut into 6 squares 2⅞″ × 2⅞″. Cut each diagonally once (E).

DARK FAT QUARTERS:
- *From each dark fat quarter:*

Cut 1 strip 15″ × width of fabric; cut into 8 pieces 1⅞″ × 15″ (F).

INNER BORDER:
Cut 6 strips 1¾″ × width of fabric.

OUTER BORDER:
Cut 8 strips 6½″ × width of fabric.

BINDING:
Cut 8 strips 2½″ × width of fabric.

piecing

Seam allowances are ¼".

1. Make 24 half-square triangles using 12 main light 3" × 3" squares (A) and 12 medium 3" × 3" squares (B). Trim the squares to 2½" × 2½". Refer to Half-Square Triangle Units (page 5).

Make 24.

2. Sew a main light triangle cut from a square 2⅞" × 2⅞" (C) to a half-square triangle from Step 1. Press in the direction of the arrow. Sew another main light triangle cut from a square 2⅞" × 2⅞" to the other side. Press in the direction of the arrow. Repeat to make a total of 12.

Make 12.

3. Sew a medium triangle cut from a square 4⅞" × 4⅞" (D) to a unit from Step 2. Press toward the medium triangle. Square the block to 4½" × 4½". Repeat to make a total of 4.

Make 4.

4. Sew the pieces from Steps 2 and 3 together. Press in the direction of the arrows. Repeat to make 4.

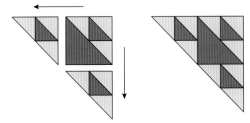

Make 4.

5. Sew 3 half-square triangles from Step 1 together with the medium triangles cut from the 2⅞" × 2⅞" (E) squares. Press in the direction of the arrows. Repeat to make 4.

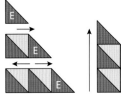

Make 4.

6. Sew the 1⅞" × 15" dark piece (F) to the piece from Step 5, centering the dark piece. Press in the direction of the arrow. Trim to create a triangle. Repeat to make 4.

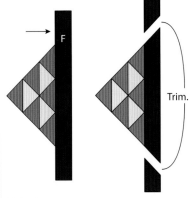

Make 4.

7. Sew the pieces from Steps 4 and 6 together to make a square. Press in the direction of the arrow. Repeat Steps 1–7 to make 4 per medium fabric for a total of 48 quarter-blocks. Square each quarter-block to 8½" × 8½".

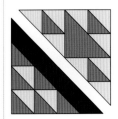 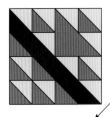

Make 4 from each medium for a total of 48 quarter-blocks.

8. Sew 4 of the various quarter-blocks together to create a block. Press in the direction of the arrows. Square the block to 16½″ × 16½″. Repeat to make the total number of blocks needed for your desired quilt size. (For the project quilt, page 29, make 12 blocks.)

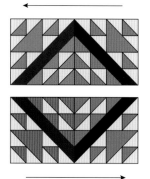

Make 12.

quilt construction

Refer to the quilt photo (page 29) and to the quilt assembly diagram (below). See Borders (page 60) for information on making the borders.

1. Arrange and sew your quilt together in rows. Press in the direction of the arrows. Sew on the inner and outer borders. Press toward the borders.

2. Quilt, bind, and enjoy!

Quilt assembly diagram

alternate quilt sizes

	Twin	Full/Queen	King
Number of blocks	15	25	36
Number of blocks wide × long	3 × 5	5 × 5	6 × 6
Finished size	62½″ × 94½″	94½″ × 94½″	110½″ × 110½″
Yardage			
Main light	2½	4¼	5¾
Medium fat quarters	15	25	36
Dark fat quarters	8	13	18
Inner border	½	½	⅝
Outer border	1⅝	2	2½
Binding	¾	⅞	1
Backing	6	8⅞	10¼ (minimum of 42″ wide)
Batting	73″ × 105″	105″ × 105″	121″ × 121″
Main light cutting			
Number of strips × width of fabric Number of squares (A)	14 strips 3″ 180 squares 3″ × 3″	24 strips 3″ 300 squares 3″ × 3″	34 strips 3″ 432 squares 3″ × 3″
Number of strips × width of fabric Number of squares (C)	14 strips 2⅞″ 180 squares 2⅞″ × 2⅞″	24 strips 2⅞″ 300 squares 2⅞″ × 2⅞″	34 strips 2⅞″ 432 squares 2⅞″ × 2⅞″

Diamonds Are Forever

Designed and made by Monique Dillard

Quilted by LeAnne Olson

Fabric: Peace on Earth by 3 Sisters for Moda Fabrics

FINISHED BLOCK: 16″ × 16″

FINISHED QUILT: 62½″ × 78½″ (12 blocks)*

* See additional information for alternate quilt sizes on page 37.

materials

- **Light fabric:** 12 fat quarters
- **Dark fabric:** 12 fat quarters
- **Inner border:** ⅜ yard
- **Outer border:** 1½ yards
- **Binding:** ⅝ yard
- **Backing:** 5⅛ yards
- **Batting:** 73″ × 89″

cutting instructions

Before cutting, match your light and dark fat quarters into pairs and cut the pairs with right sides together. Each light/dark pair makes 1 block.

LIGHT AND DARK FAT QUARTERS:
From each light and dark fat quarter:

Cut 3 strips 3″ × width of fabric; cut into 16 squares 3″ × 3″ (A and B).

Cut 1 strip 5″ × width of fabric; cut into 4 squares 5″ × 5″ (C and D).

INNER BORDER:
Cut 6 strips 1¾″ × width of fabric.

OUTER BORDER:
Cut 7 strips 6½″ × width of fabric.

BINDING:
Cut 8 strips 2½″ × width of fabric.

piecing

Seam allowances are ¼″.

1. Make 32 half-square triangles using 16 light 3″ × 3″ squares (A) and 16 dark 3″ × 3″ squares (B). Trim the squares to 2½″ × 2½″. Refer to Half-Square Triangle Units (page 5).

Make 32 from each pair.

2. Make 8 half-square triangles using 4 light 5″ × 5″ squares (C) and 4 dark 5″ × 5″ squares (D). Trim the squares to 4½″ × 4½″.

Make 8 from each pair.

3. Sew 4 of the half-square triangles from Step 1 together, mixing up the lights and darks. Press in the direction of the arrows. Square the unit to 4½″ × 4½″. Repeat to make a total of 96 units.

Make 96.

4. Sew the pieces from Step 2 and Step 3 together. Press in the direction of the arrows. Square the units to 8½″ × 8½″. Repeat to make a total of 48.

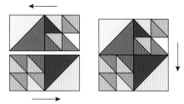

Make 48.

5. Sew the blocks together using the squares from Step 4. Press in the direction of the arrows. Square the blocks to 16½″ × 16½″. Repeat the entire procedure to make the total number of blocks needed for your desired quilt size. (For the project quilt, page 34, make 12 blocks.)

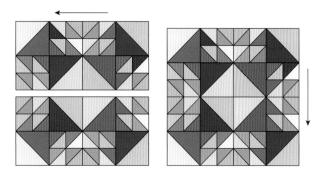

Make 12.

quilt construction

Refer to the quilt photo (page 34) and to the quilt assembly diagram (at right). See Borders (page 60) for information on making the borders.

1. Arrange and sew your quilt together in rows. Press in the direction of the arrows. Sew on the inner and outer borders. Press toward the outer border.

2. Quilt, bind, and enjoy.

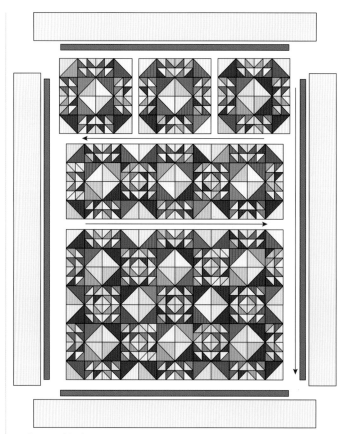

Quilt assembly diagram

alternate quilt sizes

	Twin	Full/Queen	King
Number of blocks	15	25	36
Number of blocks wide × long	3 × 5	5 × 5	6 × 6
Finished size	62½″ × 94½″	94½″ × 94½″	110½″ × 110½″
Yardage			
Light fat quarters	15	25	36
Dark fat quarters	15	25	36
Inner border	½	½	⅝
Outer border	1⅝	2	2¼
Binding	¾	⅞	1
Backing	6	8⅞	10¼
Batting	73″ × 105″	105″ × 105″	121″ × 121″

Diamond Eyes

Designed by Monique Dillard

Made and quilted by Sue Glorch

Fabric: Blueberry Hill by Blackbird Designs for Moda Fabrics

FINISHED BLOCK: 8½″ × 8½″

FINISHED QUILT: 62½″ × 81½″ (35 blocks)*

* See additional information for alternate quilt sizes on page 42.

materials

- **Main light fabric:** 3¼ yards (includes inner border and cornerstones)
- **Dark fabric:** 12 fat quarters
- **Outer border:** 1⅓ yards
- **Binding:** ⅝ yard
- **Backing:** 5¼ yards
- **Batting:** 73″ × 92″
- **Optional:** Fit to be Square ruler

cutting instructions

Each fat quarter along with the main light is enough to make 3 blocks.

MAIN LIGHT FABRIC:
From the main light fabric:

- **Fit to be Square Method (page 9)**

Cut 11 strips 5¾″ × width of fabric; cut into 72 squares 5¾″ × 5¾″ cut diagonally once (F).

Cut 9 strips 1¾″ × width of fabric; cut into 144 pieces 1¾″ × 2¼″ (D).

Cut 5 strips 2¼″ × width of fabric; cut into 72 squares 2¼″ × 2¼″ (B).

Cut 2 strips 1½″ × width of fabric; cut into 48 squares 1½″ × 1½″ (H).

Cut 7 strips 2″ × width of fabric for inner border.

- **Traditional Method (page 8)**

Cut 11 strips 5⅛″ × width of fabric; cut into 72 squares 5″ × 5″ cut diagonally once (F).

Cut 9 strips 1¾″ × width of fabric; cut into 144 pieces 1¾″ × 2¼″ (D).

Cut 5 strips 2¼″ × width of fabric; cut into 72 squares 2¼″ × 2¼″ (B).

Cut 2 strips 1½″ × width of fabric; cut into 48 squares 1½″ × 1½″ (H).

Cut 7 strips 2″ × width of fabric for inner border.

DARK FAT QUARTERS:
From each dark fat quarter:

- **Fit to be Square Method (page 9)**

Cut 2 strips 4½″ × width of fabric; cut into 6 squares 4½″ × 4½″ cut diagonally once (E), and 3 pieces 1½″ × 9″ (G).

Cut 1 strip 2¼″ × width of fabric; cut into 9 squares 2¼″ × 2¼″ (A and C).

Cut 2 strips 1½″ × width of fabric; cut into 4 pieces 1½″ × 9″ (G).

- **Traditional Method (page 8)**

Cut 2 strips 4″ × width of fabric; cut into 6 squares 4″ × 4″ cut diagonally once (E), and 3 pieces 1½″ × 9″ (G).

Cut 1 strip 2¼″ × width of fabric; cut into 9 squares 2¼″ × 2¼″ (A and C).

Cut 2 strips 1½″ × width of fabric; cut into 4 pieces 1½″ × 9″ (G).

OUTER BORDER:
Cut 7 strips 6″ × width of fabric.

BINDING:
Cut 8 strips 2½″ × width of fabric.

piecing

Seam allowances are ¼".

1. Make 12 half-square triangles using 6 main light 2¼" × 2¼" squares (B) and 6 dark 2¼" × 2¼" squares (A). Trim the squares to 1¾" × 1¾". Refer to Half-Square Triangle Units (page 5).

Make 12.

2. Sew the center of the block together using the pieces from Step 1, a dark 2¼" × 2¼" square (C), and the light 1¾" × 2¼" pieces (D). Press in the direction of the arrows. Square the block to 4¾" × 4¾". Repeat to make a total of 3 per dark fat quarter.

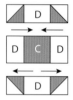

Make 3 per dark fat quarter.

3. Fit to be Square Method (page 9): Sew a dark triangle cut from a 4½" square (E) to each of 2 opposite sides of the piece from Step 2. Press toward the dark. Sew 2 more triangles of the same size to the other sides. Press toward the dark. Square the block to 6½" × 6½" using the Fit to be Square ruler. Repeat to make 3.

Traditional Method (page 8): Sew a dark triangle cut from a 4" square (E) to each of 2 opposite sides of the piece from Step 2. Press toward the dark. Sew 2 more triangles of the same size to the other sides. Press toward the dark. Square the block to 6½" × 6½". Repeat to make 3 per dark fat quarter.

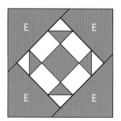

Make 3 per dark fat quarter.

4. Fit to be Square Method (page 9): Sew a light triangle cut from a 5¾" square (F) to each of 2 opposite sides of the piece from Step 3. Press toward the light. Sew 2 more of the same size triangles to the other sides. Press toward the light. Square the block to 9" × 9" using the Fit to be Square ruler. Repeat to make 3 per dark fat quarter for the total number of blocks needed for your desired quilt size. (For the project quilt, page 38, make 35 blocks. You will have an extra block left over.)

Traditional Method (page 8): Sew a light triangle cut from a 5⅛" square (F) to each of 2 opposite sides of the piece from Step 3. Press toward the light. Sew 2 more of the same size triangles to the other sides. Press toward the light. Square the block to 9" × 9". Repeat to make 3 per dark fat quarter for the total number of blocks needed for your desired quilt size. (For the project quilt, page 38, make 35 blocks. You will have an extra block left over.)

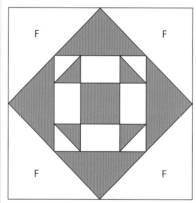

Make 3 per dark fat quarter.

quilt construction

Refer to the quilt photo (page 38) and to the quilt assembly diagram (below). See Borders (page 60) for information on making the borders.

1. Arrange and sew your quilt in rows with the dark 1½″ × 9″ pieces (G) and the main light 1½″ × 1½″ squares (H). Press toward the sashing pieces. Sew on the inner and outer borders. Press toward the borders.

2. Quilt, bind, and enjoy!

Quilt assembly diagram

alternate quilt sizes

	TWIN	FULL/QUEEN	KING
Number of blocks	40*	81	100*
Number of blocks wide × long	5 × 8	9 × 9	10 × 10
Finished size	62½″ × 91″	100½″ × 100½″	110″ × 110″
Yardage			
Main light	3¼	6⅞	8⅓
Dark fat quarters	14	27	34
Outer border	1½	1⅞	2
Binding	¾	⅞	1
Backing	5¾	9⅜	10⅛
Batting	73″ × 101″	111″ × 111″	120″ × 120″
Main light cutting: **Fit to be Square method**			
Number of strips × width of fabric Number of squares Cut diagonally into triangles (F)	12 strips 5¾″ 84 squares 5¾″ × 5¾″ Cut diagonally once.	21 strips 5¾″ 162 squares 5¾″ × 5¾″ Cut diagonally once.	30 strips 5¾″ 204 squares 5¾″ × 5¾″ Cut diagonally once.
Number of strips × width of fabric Number of pieces (D)	10 strips 1¾″ 168 pieces 1¾″ × 2¼″	20 strips 1¾″ 324 pieces 1¾″ × 2¼″	24 strips 1¾″ 408 pieces 1¾″ × 2¼″
Number of strips × width of fabric Number of squares (B)	5 strips 2¼″ 84 squares 2¼″ × 2¼″	10 strips 2¼″ 162 squares 2¼″ × 2¼″	12 strips 2¼″ 204 squares 2¼″ × 2¼″
Number of strips × width of fabric Number of squares (H)	3 strips 1½″ 54 squares 1½″ × 1½″	4 strips 1½″ 100 squares 1½″ × 1½″	5 strips 1½″ 121 squares 1½″ × 1½″
Number of strips × width of fabric For inner border	7 strips 2″	10 strips 2″	11 strips 2″
Main light cutting: **Traditional method**			
Number of strips × width of fabric Number of squares Cut diagonally into triangles (F)	11 strips 5⅛″ 84 squares 5″ × 5″ Cut diagonally once.	21 strips 5⅛″ 162 squares 5″ × 5″ Cut diagonally once.	26 strips 5⅛″ 204 squares 5″ × 5″ Cut diagonally once.
Number of strips × width of fabric Number of pieces (D)	10 strips 1¾″ 168 pieces 1¾″ × 2¼″	18 strips 1¾″ 324 pieces 1¾″ × 2¼″	24 strips 1¾″ 408 pieces 1¾″ × 2¼″
Number of strips × width of fabric Number of squares (B)	5 strips 2¼″ 84 squares 2¼″ × 2¼″	10 strips 2¼″ 162 squares 2¼″ × 2¼″	12 strips 2¼″ 204 squares 2¼″ × 2¼″
Number of strips × width of fabric Number of squares (H)	3 strips 1½″ 54 squares 1½″ × 1½″	4 strips 1½″ 100 squares 1½″ × 1½″	5 strips 1½″ 121 squares 1½″ × 1½″
Number of strips × width of fabric For inner border	7 strips 2″	10 strips 2″	11 strips 2″

You will have extra blocks.

Ocean of Diamonds

Designed by Monique Dillard

Made by Thelma Childers

Quilted by LeAnne Olson

Fabric: Memories of Provence by Monique Dillard for Maywood Studio

FINISHED BLOCK: 12″ × 12″

FINISHED QUILT: 62″ × 74″ (20 blocks)*

* See additional information for alternate quilt sizes on page 48.

materials

- **Light fabric:** 10 fat quarters
- **Blue fabric:** 10 fat quarters
- **Green fabric:** 5 fat quarters
- **Inner and outer borders:** ⅝ yard
- **Middle border:** 1⅓ yards
- **Binding:** ⅝ yard
- **Backing:** 4⅞ yards
- **Batting:** 72″ × 84″

cutting instructions

Before cutting, match your light and blue fat quarters into pairs and cut the pairs with right sides together. You will use 2 sets of blue and light fat quarters with 1 green fat quarter. Each blue and light fat-quarter pair plus half of a green fat quarter makes 2 blocks.

LIGHT FAT QUARTERS:
From each light fat quarter:

Cut 1 strip 4⅞″ × width of fabric; cut into 4 squares 4⅞″ × 4⅞″ cut diagonally once (E).

Cut 2 strips 3″ × width of fabric; cut into 8 squares 3″ × 3″ (A).

Cut 2 strips 2⅞″ × width of fabric; cut into 8 squares 2⅞″ × 2⅞″ cut diagonally once (F).

BLUE FAT QUARTERS:
From each blue fat quarter:

Cut 1 strip 4⅞″ × width of fabric; cut into 3 squares 4⅞″ × 4⅞″ cut diagonally once (G).

Cut 2 strips 3″ × width of fabric; cut into 8 squares 3″ × 3″ (B).

Cut 2 strips 2⅞″ × width of fabric; cut into 8 squares 2⅞″ × 2⅞″ cut diagonally once (D).

GREEN FAT QUARTERS:
From each green fat quarter:

Cut 1 strip 4⅞″ × width of fabric; cut into 4 squares 4⅞″ × 4⅞″ cut diagonally once (H).

Cut 2 strips 3″ × width of fabric; cut into 16 squares 3″ × 3″ (C).

INNER AND OUTER BORDERS:
Cut 14 strips 1¼″ × width of fabric.

MIDDLE BORDER:
Cut 7 strips 6″ × width of fabric.

BINDING:
Cut 8 strips 2½″ × width of fabric.

piecing

Seam allowances are ¼″.

1. Make 8 half-square triangles using 4 light 3″ × 3″ squares (A) and 4 blue 3″ × 3″ squares (B). Trim the squares to 2½″ × 2½″. Refer to Half-Square Triangle Units (page 5).

Make 8.

2. Make 8 half-square triangles using 4 light 3″ × 3″ squares (A) and 4 green 3″ × 3″ squares (C). Trim the squares to 2½″ × 2½″.

Make 8.

3. Make 8 half-square triangles using 4 blue 3″ × 3″ squares (B) and 4 green 3″ × 3″ squares (C). Trim the squares to 2½″ × 2½″.

Make 8.

4. Sew a blue triangle cut from a 2⅞″ × 2⅞″ square (D) to a half-square triangle from Step 1. Press in the direction of the arrow. Sew another blue triangle cut from a square 2⅞″ × 2⅞″ to the other side. Press in the direction of the arrow. Repeat to make a total of 4.

Make 4.

5. Sew a light triangle cut from a 4⅞″ × 4⅞″ square (E) to the piece from Step 4. Press in the direction of the arrow. Square the block to 4½″ × 4½″. Repeat to make a total of 4.

Make 4.

6. Sew a light triangle cut from a 2⅞″ × 2⅞″ square (F) to a half-square triangle from Step 2, watching the placement of the pieces. Press in the direction of the arrow. Repeat to make a total of 4.

Make 4.

7. Sew a light triangle cut from a 2⅞″ × 2⅞″ square (F) to a half-square triangle from Step 2, watching the placement of the pieces. Press in the direction of the arrow. Repeat to make a total of 4.

Make 4.

8. Sew the pieces from Steps 6 and 7 to the piece from Step 5. Press in the direction of the arrows. Repeat to make 4.

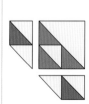

Make 4.

9. Sew a blue triangle cut from 4⅞″ × 4⅞″ square (G) to the piece from Step 8. Press in the direction of the arrows. Make 2. Square the block to 6½″ × 6½″.

Make 2.

10. Sew a green triangle cut from a 4⅞″ × 4⅞″ square (H) to the piece from Step 8. Press in the direction of the arrows. Make 2. Square the block to 6½″ × 6½″.

Make 2.

11. Sew the pieces from Steps 9 and 10 together as shown in the diagram. Square the block to 12½″ × 12½″. Repeat to make 1 block of the blue, light, and green color combination for the total number of blocks needed for your desired quilt size. (For the project quilt, page 43, make 20 blocks.)

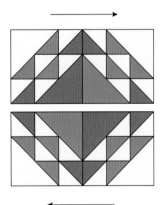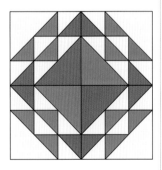

12. Sew a light triangle cut from a 2⅞″ × 2⅞″ square (F) to a half-square triangle from Step 1. Press in the direction of the arrow. Sew another dark triangle cut from a square 2⅞″ × 2⅞″ to the other side. Press in the direction of the arrow. Repeat to make a total of 4.

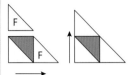

Make 4.

13. Sew a blue triangle cut from a 4⅞″ × 4⅞″ square (G) to the piece from Step 12. Press in the direction of the arrow. Square the block to 4½″ × 4½″. Repeat to make a total of 4.

Make 4.

14. Sew a blue triangle cut from a 2⅞″ × 2⅞″ square (D) to a half-square triangle from Step 3, watching the placement of the pieces. Press in the direction of the arrow. Repeat to make a total of 4.

Make 4.

15. Sew a blue triangle cut from a 2⅞″ × 2⅞″ square (D) to a half-square triangle from Step 3, watching the placement of the pieces. Press in the direction of the arrow. Repeat to make a total of 4.

Make 4.

16. Sew the pieces from Steps 14 and 15 to the piece from Step 13. Press in the direction of the arrows. Repeat to make 4.

Make 4.

17. Sew a light triangle cut from a 4⅞″ × 4⅞″ square (E) to a piece from Step 16. Press in the direction of the arrow. Make 2. Square the block to 6½″ × 6½″.

Make 2.

18. Sew a green triangle cut from a 4⅞″ × 4⅞″ square (H) to a piece from Step 16. Press in the direction of the arrow. Make 2. Square the block to 6½″ × 6½″.

Make 2.

19. Sew the blocks from Steps 17 and 18 together. Square the block to 12½″ × 12½″. Repeat to make 1 block per blue, light, and green color combination for the total number of blocks needed for your desired quilt size. (For the project quilt, page 43, make 20 blocks.)

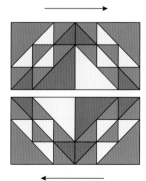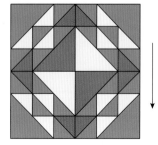

quilt construction

Refer to the quilt photo (page 43) and to the quilt assembly diagram (below). See Borders (page 60) for information on making the borders.

1. Arrange your quilt in rows and sew together. Press in the direction of the arrows. Sew on the inner, middle, and outer borders. Press toward the borders.

2. Quilt, bind, and enjoy!

Quilt assembly diagram

alternate quilt sizes

	Twin	Full/Queen	King
Number of blocks	24	56	64
Number of blocks wide × long	4 × 6	7 × 8	8 × 8
Finished size	62″ × 86″	98″ × 110″	110″ × 110″
Yardage			
Light fat quarters	12	28	32
Blue fat quarters	12	28	32
Green fat quarters	6	14	16
Inner and outer borders	¾	1	1
Middle border	1⅓	1⅞	2
Binding	¾	1	1
Backing	5½	9⅛	10⅛
Batting	72″ × 96″	108″ × 120″	120″ × 120″

Radiance

Designed by Monique Dillard

Made by Lynn Ohlendorf

Quilted by Danette Gonzalez

Fabric: Memories of Provence by Monique Dillard for Maywood Studio

FINISHED BLOCK: 10″ × 10″

FINISHED QUILT: 63″ × 83″ (35 blocks)*

See additional information for alternate quilt sizes on page 52.

materials

- **Main light fabric:** 3 yards
- **Red fabric:** 7 fat quarters
- **Black fabric:** 7 fat quarters
- **Border:** 1⅝ yards
- **Binding:** ⅝ yard
- **Backing:** 5⅓ yards
- **Batting:** 73″ × 93″
- **Optional:** Fit to be Quarter ruler

cutting instructions

Before cutting, match your red and black fat quarters together for piecing. Cut your fat quarters separately. Each pair of fat quarters along with the main light makes 5 blocks.

MAIN LIGHT FABRIC:

- **Fit to be Quarter Method (page 10)**

Cut 7 strips 3½″ × width of fabric; cut into 70 squares 3½″ × 3½″ (D).

Cut 11 strips 3″ × width of fabric; cut into 140 squares 3″ × 3″ (A).

Cut 18 strips 2½″ × width of fabric; cut into 280 squares 2½″ × 2½″ (C).

- **Traditional Method (page 10)**

Cut 6 strips 3¼″ × width of fabric; cut into 70 squares 3¼″ × 3¼″ (D).

Cut 11 strips 3″ × width of fabric; cut into 140 squares 3″ × 3″ (A).

Cut 18 strips 2½″ × width of fabric; cut into 280 squares 2½″ × 2½″ (C).

RED FAT QUARTERS:

From each red fat quarter:

Cut 4 strips 3″ × width of fabric; cut into 20 squares 3″ × 3″ (B).

BLACK FAT QUARTERS:

From each black fat quarter:

- **Fit to be Quarter Method (page 10)**

Cut 2 strips 3½″ × width of fabric; cut into 10 squares 3½″ × 3½″ (E) and 1 square 2½″ × 2½″ (F).

Cut 3 strips 2½″ × width of fabric; cut into 24 squares 2½″ × 2½″ (F).

- **Traditional Method (page 10)**

Cut 2 strips 3¼″ × width of fabric; cut into 10 squares 3¼″ × 3¼″ (E) and 1 square 2½″ × 2½″ (F).

Cut 3 strips 2½″ × width of fabric; cut into 24 squares 2½″ × 2½″ (F).

BORDER:
Cut 8 strips 7″ × width of fabric.

BINDING:
Cut 8 strips 2½″ × width of fabric.

piecing

Seam allowances are ¼".

1. Make 40 half-square triangles per red fat quarter using 20 main light 3" × 3" squares (A) and 20 red 3" × 3" squares (B). Trim the squares to 2½" × 2½". Refer to Half-Square Triangle Units (page 5).

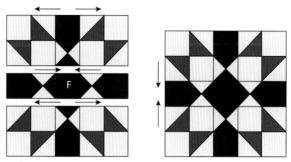

Make 40.

2. Sew 2 main light 2½" × 2½" squares (C) together with 2 half-square triangles from Step 1. Square to 4½" × 4½". Repeat to make a total of 20 per red.

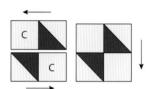

Make 20.

3. Make quarter-square triangles measuring 2½" × 2½" using main light and black.

Fit to be Quarter Method (page 10):
Use 10 black squares 3½" × 3½" (E) and 10 main light squares 3½" × 3½" (D) to make 20 quarter-square triangles per black.

Traditional Method (page 10):
Use 10 black squares 3¼" × 3¼" (E) and 10 main light squares 3¼" × 3¼" (D) to make 20 quarter-square triangles per black.

Make 20.

4. Sew the pieces from Step 3 with a black 2½" × 2½" square (F). Press toward the black square (F). Repeat to make a total of 20 per black.

Make 20.

5. Sew the blocks together in rows using the pieces from Step 2, Step 4, and a black 2½" × 2½" square (F). Press in the direction of the arrows. Repeat the entire procedure to make the total number of blocks needed for your desired quilt size. (For the project quilt, page 49, make 35 blocks.) Square the block to 10½" × 10½".

Make 5 per black and red color combination.

quilt construction

Refer to the quilt photo (page 49) and to the quilt assembly diagram (below). See Borders (page 60) for information on making the borders.

1. Arrange your quilt in rows and sew together. Rotate the blocks so that the seams are headed in opposite directions. Press in the direction of the arrows. Sew on the border. Press toward the border.

2. Quilt, bind, and enjoy!

Quilt assembly diagram

alternate quilt sizes

	Twin	Full/Queen	King
Number of blocks	40	72*	100
Number of blocks wide × long	5 × 8	8 × 9	10 × 10
Finished size	63″ × 93″	93″ × 103″	113″ × 113″
Yardage			
Main light	3⅜	6	8⅛
Red fat quarters	8	15	20
Black fat quarters	8	15	20
Border	1¾	2¼	2⅓
Binding	¾	⅞	1
Backing	5⅞	8¾	10⅜
Batting	73″ × 103″	103″ × 113″	123″ × 123″
Main light cutting: Fit to be Quarter method			
Number of strips × width of fabric Number of squares (D)	7 strips 3½″ 80 squares 3½″ × 3½″	12 strips 3½″ 144 squares 3½″ × 3½″	17 strips 3½″ 200 squares 3½″ × 3½″
Number of strips × width of fabric Number of squares (A)	13 strips 3″ 160 squares 3″ × 3″	23 strips 3″ 288 squares 3″ × 3″	31 strips 3″ 400 squares 3″ × 3″
Number of strips × width of fabric Number of squares (C)	20 strips 2½″ 320 squares 2½″ × 2½″	36 strips 2½″ 576 squares 2½″ × 2½″	50 strips 2½″ 800 squares 2½″ × 2½″
Main light cutting: Traditional method			
Number of strips × width of fabric Number of squares (D)	7 strips 3¼″ 80 squares 3¼″ × 3¼″	12 strips 3¼″ 144 squares 3¼″ × 3¼″	17 strips 3¼″ 200 squares 3¼″ × 3¼″
Number of strips × width of fabric Number of squares (A)	13 strips 3″ 160 squares 3″ × 3″	23 strips 3″ 288 squares 3″ × 3″	31 strips 3″ 400 squares 3″ × 3″
Number of strips × width of fabric Number of squares (C)	20 strips 2½″ 320 squares 2½″ × 2½″	36 strips 2½″ 576 squares 2½″ × 2½″	50 strips 2½″ 800 squares 2½″ × 2½″

You will have extra blocks.

Blue Heart Diamond

Designed by Monique Dillard

Made by Peggy Drake

Quilted by Danette Gonzalez

Fabric: Prairie Paisley II by Minick & Simpson for Moda Fabrics

FINISHED BLOCK: 12″ × 12″

FINISHED QUILT: 50″ × 62″ (12 blocks)*

* See additional information for alternate quilt sizes on page 56.

materials

- **Light fabric:** 6 fat quarters
- **Dark fabric:** 12 fat quarters
- **Inner border:** ¼ yard
- **Outer border:** 1⅜ yards
- **Binding:** ½ yard
- **Backing:** 3½ yards
- **Batting:** 60″ × 72″
- **Optional:** Fit to be Geese ruler and Fit to be Quarter ruler

cutting instructions

Each dark fat quarter along with half of a light fat quarter makes 1 block.

LIGHT FAT QUARTERS:
From each light fat quarter:

- **Fit to be Geese Method (page 7) and Fit to be Quarter Method (page 6)**

Cut 1 strip 5½″ × width of fabric; cut into 2 squares 5½″ × 5½″ cut diagonally twice (B) and 4 pieces 2¾″ × 3¾″ (D).

Cut 2 strips 3¼″ × width of fabric; cut into 8 squares 3¼″ × 3¼″ cut diagonally once (H).

Cut 1 strip 2¾″ × width of fabric; cut into 4 pieces 2¾″ × 3¾″ (D).

Cut 1 strip 2½″ × width of fabric; cut into 8 squares 2½″ × 2½″ (F).

- **Traditional Method (pages 7 and 5)**

Cut 1 strip 4½″ × width of fabric; cut into 8 pieces 2½″ × 4½″ (B).

Cut 1 strip 3½″ × width of fabric; cut into 8 pieces 3½″ × 2½″ (D).

Cut 3 strips 2½″ × width of fabric; cut into 24 squares 2½″ × 2½″ (H and F).

DARK FAT QUARTERS:
From each dark fat quarter:

- **Fit to be Geese Method (page 7) and Fit to be Quarter Method (page 6)**

Cut 1 strip 6″ × width of fabric; cut into 2 pieces 6″ × 5″ (J), 1 square 5½″ × 5½″ cut diagonally twice (G), and 1 square 4½″ × 4½″ (I).

Cut 1 strip 3¼″ × width of fabric; cut into 4 squares 3¼″ × 3¼″ cut diagonally once (A).

Cut 1 strip 2¾″ × width of fabric; cut into 4 squares 2¾″ × 2¾″ (C).

- **Traditional Method (pages 7 and 5)**

Cut 1 strip 4½″ × width of fabric; cut into 2 pieces 4½″ × 5½″ (J) and 1 square 4½″ × 4½″ (I).

Cut 3 strips 2½″ × width of fabric; cut into 12 squares 2½″ × 2½″ (A and C) and 4 pieces 2½″ × 4½″ (G).

INNER BORDER:
Cut 5 strips 1½″ × width of fabric.

OUTER BORDER:
Cut 6 strips 6½″ × width of fabric.

BINDING:
Cut 7 strips 2½″ × width of fabric.

piecing

Seam allowances are ¼".

1. Make 48 Flying Geese units measuring 2½" × 4½" from the various light and dark fat quarters.

> **Fit to be Geese Method (page 7):** Use 96 dark triangles cut from 3¼" × 3¼" squares cut diagonally once (A) and 48 light triangles cut from 5½" × 5½" squares cut diagonally twice (B).

> **Traditional Method (page 7):** Use 96 dark 2½" × 2½" squares (A) and 48 light 2½" × 4½" pieces (B).

Make 48.

2. Make 48 Flying Geese units measuring 2½" × 4½" from the various light and dark fat quarters.

> **Fit to be Geese Method (page 7):** Use 96 light triangles cut from 3¼" × 3¼" squares cut diagonally once (G) and 48 dark triangles cut from 5½" × 5½" squares cut diagonally twice (H).

> **Traditional Method (page 7):** Use 96 light 2½" × 2½" squares (G) and 48 dark 2½" × 4½" pieces (H).

Make 48.

3. Sew the pieces from Steps 1 and 2 together as shown in the diagram. Press in the direction of the arrow. Repeat to make 48.

Make 48.

4. Make 48 combination units measuring 4½" × 4½" from the various light and dark fat quarters.

> **Fit to be Quarter Method (page 6):** Use 48 light 2¾" × 3¾" pieces (D), 48 dark 2¾" × 2¾" squares (C), and 24 dark 6" × 5" pieces (J).

Traditional Method (page 5): Use 48 light 2½" × 3½" pieces (D), 48 dark 2½" × 2½" squares (C), and 24 dark 4½" × 5½" pieces (J).

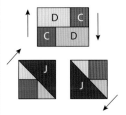

Make 48.

5. On the back of 48 light 2½" × 2½" squares (F), draw a diagonal line from corner to corner. Place a drawn square with right sides together on a dark 4½" × 4½" square (I). Sew exactly on the line and press in the direction of the arrow. Trim the bottom layers to ¼". Sew another drawn light 2½" × 2½" square (F) on the opposite corner. Press in the direction of the arrow. Place 2 more drawn light 2½" × 2½" squares (F) on the opposite corners of the piece you just made. Sew exactly on the line and press in the direction of the arrows. Trim the bottom layers to ¼". Square to 4½" × 4½". Make a total of 12.

Make 12.

6. Sew the block together in rows using the pieces from Steps 3–5. Press in the direction of the arrows. Square to 12½" × 12½". Repeat the entire procedure to make the total number of blocks needed for your desired quilt size. (For the project quilt, page 53, make 12 blocks.)

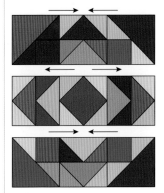 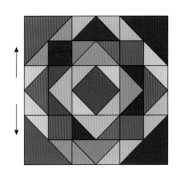

Make 12.

quilt construction

Refer to the quilt photo (page 53) and to the quilt assembly diagram (at right). See Borders (page 60) for information on making the borders.

1. Arrange and sew your quilt together in rows. Rotate block so that seams head in opposite directions. Press in the direction of the arrows. Sew on the inner and outer borders. Press toward the borders.

2. Quilt, bind, and enjoy!

Quilt assembly diagram

alternate quilt sizes

	Twin	Full/Queen	King
Number of blocks	24	56	64
Number of blocks wide × long	4 × 6	7 × 8	8 × 8
Finished size	62″ × 86″	98″ × 110″	110″ × 110″
Yardage			
Light fat quarters	12	28	32
Dark fat quarters	24	56	64
Inner border	⅓	½	½
Outer border	1½	2¼	2¼
Binding	¾	1	1
Backing	5½	9⅛	10⅛
Batting	72″ × 96″	108″ × 120″	120″ × 120″

Brilliance

Designed and made by Monique Dillard

Quilted by LeAnne Olson

Fabric: Lost & Found by My Mind's Eye for Riley Blake

FINISHED BLOCKS: 5½″ × 5½″ and 5½″ × 11″

FINISHED QUILT: 39″ × 50″ (32 blocks)

materials

- **Light fabric:** 4 fat quarters
- **Dark fabric:** 4 fat quarters
- **Print fabric:** 8 fat quarters
- **Border:** ⅔ yard
- **Binding:** ½ yard
- **Backing:** 2⅞ yards
- **Batting:** 49″ × 60″

cutting instructions

LIGHT FAT QUARTERS:
From each light fat quarter:

Cut 15 strips 1″ × width of fabric; cut into 16 pieces 1″ × 6″ (C), 8 pieces 1″ × 10½″ (E), and 8 pieces 1″ × 5″ (A).

DARK FAT QUARTERS:
From each dark fat quarter:

Cut 4 strips 2¼″ × width of fabric; cut into 32 squares 2¼″ × 2¼″ (D).

PRINT FAT QUARTERS:
From each print fat quarter:

Cut 2 strips 5″ × width of fabric; cut into 2 pieces 5″ × 10½″ (F) and 2 squares 5″ × 5″ (B).

BORDER:
Cut 5 strips 3½″ × width of fabric.

BINDING:
Cut 5 strips 2½″ × width of fabric.

piecing

Seam allowances are ¼″.

1. Sew a light 1″ × 5″ piece (A) to opposite sides of a print 5″ × 5″ square (B). Press toward the light. Sew a light 1″ × 6″ piece (C) to the top and bottom. Press toward the light. Repeat for all 5″ × 5″ squares for a total of 16.

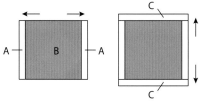

Make 16.

2. On the back of the dark 2¼″ × 2¼″ squares (D), draw a diagonal line from corner to corner. Place a drawn square on the corner of the pieces from Step 1 and sew on the drawn line. Sew 3 more squares of the same size on the remaining corners. Press 2 in and 2 out. Trim the bottom 2 layers to ¼″. Repeat to make 16 for the project quilt (page 57) or the total number needed for your desired quilt size.

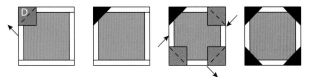

Make 16.

3. Sew a light 1″ × 10½″ piece (E) to opposite sides of a print 5″ × 10½″ piece (F). Press toward the light. Sew a light 1″ × 6″ piece (C) to the top and bottom. Press toward the light. Repeat for all 5″ × 10½″ pieces for a total of 16.

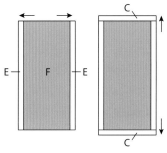

Make 16.

4. Place a drawn square (D) from Step 2 on the corner of the pieces from Step 3 and sew on the drawn line. Sew 3 more squares on the remaining corners. Press 2 in and 2 out. Trim the bottom 2 layers to ¼″. Repeat to make 16 for the project quilt (page 57) or the total number needed for your desired quilt size.

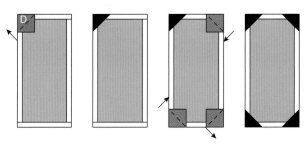

Make 16.

quilt construction

Refer to the quilt photo (page 57) and to the quilt assembly diagram (below). See Borders (page 60) for information on making the borders.

1. Arrange your quilt as shown and sew together. Press in the direction of the arrows. Sew on the border. Press toward the border.

2. Quilt, bind, and enjoy!

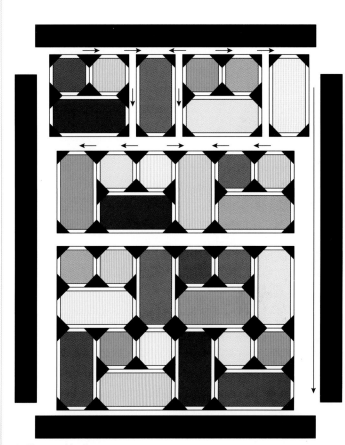

Quilt assembly diagram

Quiltmaking Basics

general guidelines

seam allowances

A ¼" seam allowance is used for most projects. It's a good idea to do a test seam before you begin sewing to check that your ¼" is accurate. Accuracy is the key to successful piecing.

pressing

In general, press seams toward the darker fabric. Press lightly in an up-and-down motion. Avoid using a very hot iron or over-ironing, which can distort shapes and blocks. Be especially careful when pressing bias edges because they stretch easily.

borders

When border strips are cut on the crosswise grain, piece the strips together to achieve the needed lengths.

butted borders

In most cases the side borders are sewn on first. When you have finished the quilt top, measure it through the center vertically. This will be the length to cut the side borders. Place pins at the centers of all four sides of the quilt top, as well as in the center of each side border strip. Pin the side borders to the quilt top first, matching the center pins. Using a ¼" seam allowance, sew the borders to the quilt top and press toward the border.

Next, measure horizontally across the center of the quilt top, including the side borders. This will be the length to cut the top and bottom borders. Repeat, pinning, sewing, and pressing.

backing

Plan on making the backing a minimum of 8" longer and wider than the quilt top. Piece, if necessary. Trim the selvages before you piece to the desired size.

batting

The type of batting to use is a personal decision; consult your local quilt shop. Cut batting approximately 10" longer and wider than your quilt top. Note that your batting choice will affect how much quilting is necessary for the quilt. Check the manufacturer's instructions to see how far apart the quilting lines can be.

basting

Basting keeps the quilt "sandwich" layers from shifting while you are quilting.

If you plan to machine quilt, pin baste the quilt layers together with safety pins placed a minimum of 3"–4" apart. Begin basting in the center and move toward the edges, first in vertical, then horizontal, rows. Try not to pin directly on the intended quilting lines.

If you plan to hand quilt, baste the layers together with thread using a long needle and light-colored thread. Knot one end of the thread. Using stitches approximately the length of the needle, begin in the center and move out toward the edges in vertical and horizontal rows approximately 4" apart. Add two diagonal rows of basting.

binding

Trim excess batting and backing from the quilt even with the edges of the quilt top.

double-fold straight-grain binding

If you want a ¼″ finished binding, cut the binding strips 2½″ wide and piece them together with diagonal seams to make a continuous binding strip. Trim the seam allowance to ¼″. Press the seams open.

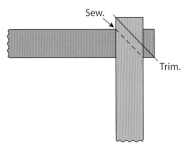

Sew from corner to corner.

Completed diagonal seam

Press the entire strip in half lengthwise with wrong sides together. With raw edges even, pin the binding to the front edge of the quilt a few inches away from the corner, and leave the first few inches of the binding unattached. Start sewing, using a ¼″ seam allowance.

Stop ¼″ away from the first corner (see Step 1) and back-stitch one stitch. Lift the presser foot and needle. Rotate the quilt one-quarter turn. Fold the binding at a right angle so it extends straight above the quilt and the fold forms a 45° angle in the corner (see Step 2). Then bring the binding strip down even with the edge of the quilt (see Step 3). Begin sewing at the folded edge. Repeat in the same manner at all corners.

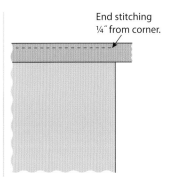

Step 1. Stitch to ¼″ from corner.

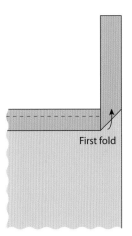

Step 2. First fold for miter

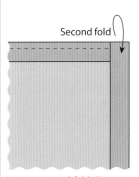

Step 3. Second fold alignment

Continue stitching until you are back near the beginning of the binding strip. See Finishing the Binding Ends for tips on finishing and hiding the raw edges of the ends of the binding.

finishing the binding ends

METHOD 1

After stitching around the quilt, fold under the beginning tail of the binding strip ¼" so that the raw edge will be inside the binding after it is turned to the backside of the quilt. Place the end tail of the binding strip over the beginning folded end. Continue to attach the binding and stitch slightly beyond the starting stitches. Trim the excess binding. Fold the binding over the raw edges to the quilt back and hand stitch, mitering the corners.

METHOD 2

Fold the ending tail of the binding back on itself where it meets the beginning binding tail. From the fold, measure and mark the cut width of your binding strip. Cut the ending binding tail to this measurement. For example, if your binding is cut 2½" wide, measure from the fold on the ending tail of the binding 2⅛" and cut the binding tail to this length.

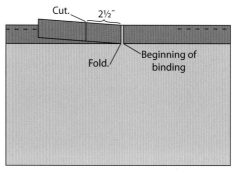

Cut binding tail.

Open both tails. Place one tail on top of the other tail at right angles, right sides together. Mark a diagonal line from corner to corner and stitch on the line. Check that you've done it correctly and that the binding fits the quilt; then trim the seam allowance to ¼". Press open.

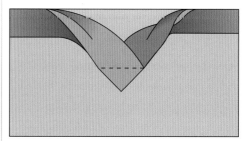

Stitch ends of binding diagonally.

Refold the binding and stitch this binding section in place on the quilt. Fold the binding over the raw edges to the quilt back and hand stitch.

Note: For a short video on this technique, go to www.ctpub.com. Scroll down to the bottom of the page to Consumer Resources and click the link to Quiltmaking Basics. Select Completing a Binding with an Invisible Seam.

About the Author

Monique Dillard of Rockford, Illinois, was born in Winnipeg, Manitoba, Canada. Her love of quilting was nurtured by relatives in Canada who taught her the art of handwork and sewing. She parlayed her degree in mathematics into a genuine understanding of the need for accurate ¼" seams, squared blocks, and precise cutting. She was a regular teacher at her local quilt shop for 15 years until her budding quilt design business, Open Gate, steered her career toward a national audience. These days, you can find Monique teaching across the United States at quilt guilds, quilt shops, and weekend retreats. Monique's classes always fill up fast with fans from previous classes and students eager to learn from this talented designer.

Follow Monique at www.opengatequilts.com as she continues to create unique and creative quilt patterns, books, and rulers.

Resources

Fit to be Geese Ruler, Fit to be Quarter Ruler, and Fit to be Square Ruler are available for wholesale and retail sales through www.opengatequilts.com.

Monique Dillard
1607 Charlotte Drive
Rockford, IL 61108

Fabrics used in these projects:

Riley Blake fabric www.rileyblakedesigns.com

Moda fabrics www.unitednotions.com

Maywood Studio fabrics www.maywoodstudio.com

Batik fabrics www.hoffmanfabrics.com

RJR fabrics www.rjrfabrics.com

ALSO BY MONIQUE DILLARD:

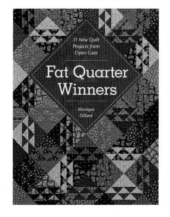

Great Titles *from* C&T PUBLISHING

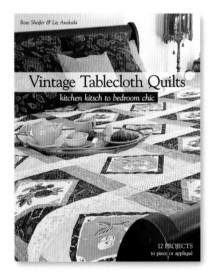

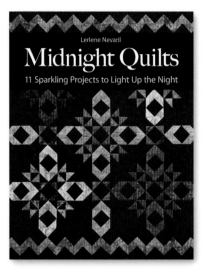

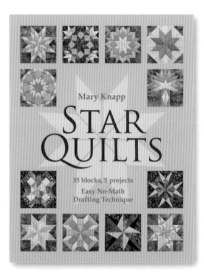

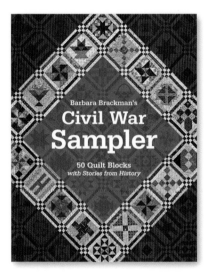

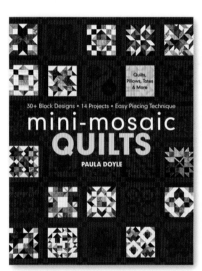

Available at your local retailer or **www.ctpub.com** *or* **800-284-1114**

For a list of other fine books from C&T Publishing, visit our website
to view our catalog online.

C&T PUBLISHING, INC.

P.O. Box 1456
Lafayette, CA 94549
800-284-1114

Email: ctinfo@ctpub.com
Website: www.ctpub.com

C&T Publishing's professional photography services are now available to
the public. Visit us at www.ctmediaservices.com.

Tips and Techniques can be found at www.ctpub.com > Consumer
Resources > Quiltmaking Basics: Tips & Techniques for Quiltmaking & More

For quilting supplies:

COTTON PATCH

1025 Brown Ave.
Lafayette, CA 94549
Store: 925-284-1177
Mail order: 925-283-7883

Email: CottonPa@aol.com
Website: www.quiltusa.com

Note: Fabrics shown may not be currently available, as fabric
manufacturers keep most fabrics in print for only a short time.